A SHROPSHIRE LAD

POEMS BY A. E. HOUSMAN

With decorations in color by EDWARD A. WILSON
& an appendix of bibliographic material gathered
by CARL J. WEBER : New York, The Heritage Press

A SHROPSHIRE LAD

POEMS BY A. E. HOUSMAN

A LIST OF THE POEMS

A SHROPSHIRE LAD

POEMS BY A. E. HOUSMAN

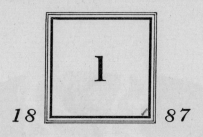

1

1887

From Clee to heaven the beacon burns,
The shires have seen it plain,
From north and south the sign returns
And beacons burn again.

Look left, look right, the hills are bright,
The dales are light between,
Because 'tis fifty years to-night
That God has saved the Queen.

Now, when the flame they watch not towers
Above the soil they trod,
Lads, we'll remember friends of ours
Who shared the work with God.

To skies that knit their heartstrings right,
To fields that bred them brave,

The saviours come not home to-night:
Themselves they could not save.

It dawns in Asia, tombstones show
And Shropshire names are read;
And the Nile spills his overflow
Beside the Severn's dead.

We pledge in peace by farm and town
The Queen they served in war,
And fire the beacons up and down
The land they perished for.

'God save the Queen' we living sing,
From height to height 'tis heard;
And with the rest your voices ring,
Lads of the Fifty-third.

Oh, God will save her, fear you not:
Be you the men you've been,
Get you the sons your fathers got,
And God will save the Queen.

2

Loveliest of trees, the cherry now
Is hung with bloom along the bough,
And stands about the woodland ride
Wearing white for Eastertide.

Now, of my threescore years and ten,
Twenty will not come again,
And take from seventy springs a score,
It only leaves me fifty more.

And since to look at things in bloom
Fifty springs are little room,
About the woodlands I will go
To see the cherry hung with snow.

THE RECRUIT

Leave your home behind, lad,
And reach your friends your hand,
And go, and luck go with you
While Ludlow tower shall stand.

Oh, come you home of Sunday
When Ludlow streets are still
And Ludlow bells are calling
To farm and lane and mill,

Or come you home of Monday
When Ludlow market hums
And Ludlow chimes are playing
'The conquering hero comes,'

Come you home a hero,
Or come not home at all,
The lads you leave will mind you
Till Ludlow tower shall fall.

And you will list the bugle
That blows in lands of morn,
And make the foes of England
Be sorry you were born.

And you till trump of doomsday
On lands of morn may lie,
And make the hearts of comrades
Be heavy where you die.

Leave your home behind you,
Your friends by field and town:
Oh, town and field will mind you
Till Ludlow tower is down.

REVEILLE

Wake: the silver dusk returning
Up the beach of darkness brims,
And the ship of sunrise burning
Strands upon the eastern rims.

Wake: the vaulted shadow shatters,
Trampled to the floor it spanned,
And the tent of night in tatters
Straws the sky-pavilioned land.

Up, lad, up, 'tis late for lying:
Hear the drums of morning play;
Hark, the empty highways crying
'Who'll beyond the hills away?'

Towns and countries woo together,
Forelands beacon, belfries call;
Never lad that trod on leather
Lived to feast his heart with all.

Up, lad: thews that lie and cumber
Sunlit pallets never thrive;
Morns abed and daylight slumber
Were not meant for man alive.

Clay lies still, but blood's a rover;
Breath's a ware that will not keep.
Up, lad: when the journey's over
There'll be time enough to sleep.

5

Oh see how thick the goldcup flowers
Are lying in field and lane,
With dandelions to tell the hours
That never are told again.
Oh may I squire you round the meads
And pick you posies gay?
—'Twill do no harm to take my arm.
'You may, young man, you may.'

Ah, spring was sent for lass and lad,
'Tis now the blood runs gold,
And man and maid had best be glad
Before the world is old.
What flowers to-day may flower to-morrow,
But never as good as new.
—Suppose I wound my arm right round—
''Tis true, young man, 'tis true.'

Some lads there are, 'tis shame to say,
That only court to thieve,
And once they bear the bloom away
'Tis little enough they leave.
Then keep your heart for men like me
And safe from trustless chaps.
My love is true and all for you.
'Perhaps, young man, perhaps.'

Oh, look in my eyes then, can you doubt?
—Why, 'tis a mile from town.
How green the grass is all about!
We might as well sit down.
—Ah, life, what is it but a flower?
Why must true lovers sigh?
Be kind, have pity, my own, my pretty,—
'Good-bye, young man, good-bye.'

6

When the lad for longing sighs,
Mute and dull of cheer and pale,
If at death's own door he lies,
Maiden, you can heal his ail.

Lovers' ills are all to buy:
The wan look, the hollow tone,
The hung head, the sunken eye,
You can have them for your own.

Buy them, buy them: eve and morn
Lovers' ills are all to sell.
Then you can lie down forlorn;
But the lover will be well.

7

When smoke stood up from Ludlow,
And mist blew off from Teme,
And blithe afield to ploughing
Against the morning beam
I strode beside my team,

The blackbird in the coppice
Looked out to see me stride,
And hearkened as I whistled
The trampling team beside,
And fluted and replied:

'Lie down, lie down, young yeoman;
What use to rise and rise?
Rise man a thousand mornings
Yet down at last he lies,
And then the man is wise.'

I heard the tune he sang me,
And spied his yellow bill;
I picked a stone and aimed it
And threw it with a will:
Then the bird was still.

Then my soul within me
Took up the blackbird's strain,
And still beside the horses
Along the dewy lane
It sang the song again:

'Lie down, lie down, young yeoman;
The sun moves always west;
The road one treads to labour
Will lead one home to rest,
And that will be the best.'

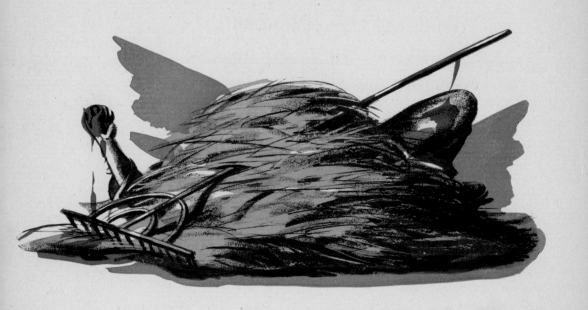

┌─────────────┐
│   │
│   8   │
│   │
└─────────────┘

'Farewell to barn and stack and tree,
Farewell to Severn shore.
Terence, look your last at me,
For I come home no more.

'The sun burns on the half-mown hill,
By now the blood is dried;
And Maurice amongst the hay lies still
And my knife is in his side.

'My mother thinks us long away;
'Tis time the field were mown.
She had two sons at rising day,
To-night she'll be alone.

'And here's a bloody hand to shake,
And oh, man, here's good-bye;
We'll sweat no more on scythe and rake,
My bloody hands and I.

'I wish you strength to bring you pride,
And a love to keep you clean,
And I wish you luck, come Lammastide,
At racing on the green.

'Long for me the rick will wait,
And long will wait the fold,
And long will stand the empty plate,
And dinner will be cold.'

On moonlit heath and lonesome bank
The sheep beside me graze;
And yon the gallows used to clank
Fast by the four cross ways.

A careless shepherd once would keep
The flocks by moonlight there,
And high amongst the glimmering sheep
The dead man stood on air.

They hang us now in Shrewsbury jail:
The whistles blow forlorn,
And trains all night groan on the rail
To men that die at morn.

There sleeps in Shrewsbury jail to-night,
Or wakes, as may betide,

A better lad, if things went right,
Than most that sleep outside.

And naked to the hangman's noose
The morning clocks will ring
A neck God made for other use
Than strangling in a string.

And sharp the link of life will snap,
And dead on air will stand
Heels that held up as straight a chap
As treads upon the land.

So here I'll watch the night and wait
To see the morning shine,
When he will hear the stroke of eight
And not the stroke of nine;

And wish my friend as sound a sleep
As lads' I did not know,
That shepherded the moonlit sheep
A hundred years ago.

MARCH

The Sun at noon to higher air,
Unharnessing the silver Pair
That late before his chariot swam,
Rides on the gold wool of the Ram.

So braver notes the storm-cock sings
To start the rusted wheel of things,
And brutes in field and brutes in pen
Leap that the world goes round again.

The boys are up the woods with day
To fetch the daffodils away,
And home at noonday from the hills
They bring no dearth of daffodils.

Afield for palms the girls repair,
And sure enough the palms are there,
And each will find by hedge or pond
Her waving silver-tufted wand.

In farm and field through all the shire
The eye beholds the heart's desire;
Ah, let not only mine be vain,
For lovers should be loved again.

11

On your midnight pallet lying,
Listen, and undo the door:
Lads that waste the light in sighing
In the dark should sigh no more;
Night should ease a lover's sorrow;
Therefore, since I go to-morrow,
Pity me before.

In the land to which I travel,
The far dwelling, let me say—
Once, if here the couch is gravel,
In a kinder bed I lay,
And the breast the darnel smothers
Rested once upon another's
When it was not clay.

12

When I watch the living meet,
And the moving pageant file
Warm and breathing through the street
Where I lodge a little while,
If the heats of hate and lust
In the house of flesh are strong,
Let me mind the house of dust
Where my sojourn shall be long.

In the nation that is not
Nothing stands that stood before;
There revenges are forgot,
And the hater hates no more;
Lovers lying two and two
Ask not whom they sleep beside,
And the bridegroom all night through
Never turns him to the bride.

13

When I was one-and-twenty
I heard a wise man say,
'Give crowns and pounds and guineas
But not your heart away;
Give pearls away and rubies
But keep your fancy free.'
But I was one-and-twenty,
No use to talk to me.

When I was one-and-twenty
I heard him say again,
'The heart out of the bosom
Was never given in vain;
'Tis paid with sighs a plenty
And sold for endless rue.'
And I am two-and-twenty,
And oh, 'tis true, 'tis true.

14

There pass the careless people
That call their souls their own;
Here by the road I loiter,
How idle and alone.

Ah, past the plunge of plummet,
In seas I cannot sound,
My heart and soul and senses,
World without end, are drowned.

His folly has not fellow
Beneath the blue of day
That gives to man or woman
His heart and soul away.

There flowers no balm to sain him
From east of earth to west
That's lost for everlasting
The heart out of his breast.

Here by the labouring highway
With empty hands I stroll:
Sea-deep, till doomsday morning,
Lie lost my heart and soul.

15

Look not in my eyes, for fear
They mirror true the sight I see,
And there you find your face too clear
And love it and be lost like me.
One the long nights through must lie
Spent in star-defeated sighs,
But why should you as well as I
Perish? gaze not in my eyes.

A Grecian lad, as I hear tell,
One that many loved in vain,
Looked into a forest well
And never looked away again.
There, when the turf in springtime flowers,
With downward eye and gazes sad,
Stands amid the glancing showers
A jonquil, not a Grecian lad.

16

It nods and curtseys and recovers
When the wind blows above,
The nettle on the graves of lovers
That hanged themselves for love.

The nettle nods, the wind blows over,
The man, he does not move,
The lover of the grave, the lover
That hanged himself for love.

17

Twice a week the winter thorough
Here stood I to keep the goal:
Football then was fighting sorrow
For the young man's soul.

Now in Maytime to the wicket
Out I march with bat and pad:
See the son of grief at cricket
Trying to be glad.

Try I will: no harm in trying:
Wonder 'tis how little mirth
Keeps the bones of man from lying
On the bed of earth.

18

Oh, when I was in love with you,
Then I was clean and brave,
And miles around the wonder grew
How well did I behave.

And now the fancy passes by,
And nothing will remain,
And miles around they'll say that I
Am quite myself again.

TO AN ATHLETE DYING YOUNG

The time you won your town the race
We chaired you through the market-place;
Man and boy stood cheering by,
And home we brought you shoulder-high.

To-day, the road all runners come,
Shoulder-high we bring you home,
And set you at your threshold down,
Townsman of a stiller town.

Smart lad, to slip betimes away
From fields where glory does not stay
And early though the laurel grows
It withers quicker than the rose.

Eyes the shady night has shut
Cannot see the record cut,
And silence sounds no worse than cheers
After earth has stopped the ears:

Now you will not swell the rout
Of lads that wore their honours out,
Runners whom renown outran
And the name died before the man.

So set, before its echoes fade,
The fleet foot on the sill of shade,
And hold to the low lintel up
The still-defended challenge-cup.

And round that early-laurelled head
Will flock to gaze the strengthless dead,
And find unwithered on its curls
The garland briefer than a girl's.

20

Oh fair enough are sky and plain,
But I know fairer far:
Those are as beautiful again
That in the water are;
The pools and rivers wash so clean
The trees and clouds and air,
The like on earth was never seen,
And oh that I were there.

These are the thoughts I often think
As I stand gazing down
In act upon the cressy brink
To strip and dive and drown;
But in the golden-sanded brooks
And azure meres I spy
A silly lad that longs and looks
And wishes he were I.

BREDON HILL

In summertime on Bredon
The bells they sound so clear;
Round both the shires they ring them
In steeples far and near,
A happy noise to hear.

Here of a Sunday morning
My love and I would lie,
And see the coloured counties,
And hear the larks so high
About us in the sky.

The bells would ring to call her
In valleys miles away:

'Come all to church, good people;
Good people, come and pray.'
But here my love would stay.

And I would turn and answer
Among the springing thyme,
'Oh, peal upon our wedding,
And we will hear the chime,
And come to church in time.'

But when the snows at Christmas
On Bredon top were strown,
My love rose up so early
And stole out unbeknown
And went to church alone.

They tolled the one bell only,
Groom there was none to see,
The mourners followed after,
And so to church went she,
And would not wait for me.

The bells they sound on Bredon,
And still the steeples hum.
'Come all to church, good people,'—
Oh, noisy bells, be dumb;
I hear you, I will come.

22

The street sounds to the soldiers' tread,
And out we troop to see:
A single redcoat turns his head,
He turns and looks at me.

My man, from sky to sky's so far,
We never crossed before;
Such leagues apart the world's ends are.
We're like to meet no more;

What thoughts at heart have you and I
We cannot stop to tell;
But dead or living, drunk or dry,
Soldier, I wish you well.

23

The lads in their hundreds to Ludlow come in for
    the fair,
There's men from the barn and the forge and the
    mill and the fold,
The lads for the girls and the lads for the liquor
    are there,
And there with the rest are the lads that will
    never be old.

There's chaps from the town and the field and the
    till and the cart,
And many to count are the stalwart, and many
    the brave,
And many the handsome of face and the hand-
    some of heart,
And few that will carry their looks or their truth
    to the grave.

I wish one could know them, I wish there were
  tokens to tell
The fortunate fellows that now you can never
  discern;
And then one could talk with them friendly and
  wish them farewell
And watch them depart on the way that they will
  not return.

But now you may stare as you like and there's
  nothing to scan;
And brushing your elbow unguessed-at and not
  to be told
They carry back bright to the coiner the mintage
  of man,
The lads that will die in their glory and never be
  old.

24

Say, lad, have you things to do?
Quick then, while your day's at prime.
Quick, and if 'tis work for two,
Here am I, man: now's your time.

Send me now, and I shall go;
Call me, I shall hear you call;
Use me ere they lay me low
Where a man's no use at all;

Ere the wholesome flesh decay,
And the willing nerve be numb,
And the lips lack breath to say,
'No, my lad, I cannot come.'

25

This time of year a twelvemonth past,
When Fred and I would meet,
We needs must jangle, till at last
We fought and I was beat.
So then the summer fields about,
Till rainy days began,
Rose Harland on her Sundays out
Walked with the better man.

The better man she walks with still,
Though now 'tis not with Fred.
A lad that lives and has his will
Is worth a dozen dead.
Fred keeps the house all kinds of weather,
And clay's the house he keeps;
When Rose and I walk out together
Stock-still lies Fred and sleeps.

26

Along the field as we came by
A year ago, my love and I,
The aspen over stile and stone
Was talking to itself alone.
'Oh who are these that kiss and pass?
A country lover and his lass;
Two lovers looking to be wed;
And time shall put them both to bed,
But she shall lie with earth above,
And he beside another love.'

And sure enough beneath the tree
There walks another love with me,
And overhead the aspen heaves
Its rainy-sounding silver leaves;
And I spell nothing in their stir,

But now perhaps they speak to her,
And plain for her to understand
They talk about a time at hand
When I shall sleep with clover clad,
And she beside another lad.

27

'Is my team ploughing,
That I was used to drive
And hear the harness jingle
When I was man alive?'

Ay, the horses trample,
The harness jingles now;
No change though you lie under
The land you used to plough.

'Is football playing
Along the river shore,
With lads to chase the leather,
Now I stand up no more?'

Ay, the ball is flying,
The lads play heart and soul;

The goal stands up, the keeper
Stands up to keep the goal.

'Is my girl happy,
That I thought hard to leave,
And has she tired of weeping
As she lies down at eve?'

Ay, she lies down lightly,
She lies not down to weep:
Your girl is well contented.
Be still, my lad, and sleep.

'Is my friend hearty,
Now I am thin and pine,
And has he found to sleep in
A better bed than mine?'

Yes, lad, I lie easy,
I lie as lads would choose;
I cheer a dead man's sweetheart,
Never ask me whose.

28

THE WELSH MARCHES

High the vanes of Shrewsbury gleam
Islanded in Severn stream;
The bridges from the steepled crest
Cross the water east and west.

The flag of morn in conqueror's state
Enters at the English gate:
The vanquished eve, as night prevails,
Bleeds upon the road to Wales.

Ages since the vanquished bled
Round my mother's marriage-bed;
There the ravens feasted far
About the open house of war:

When Severn down to Buildwas ran
Coloured with the death of man,
Couched upon her brother's grave
The Saxon got me on the slave.

The sound of fight is silent long
That began the ancient wrong;
Long the voice of tears is still
That wept of old the endless ill.

In my heart it has not died,
The war that sleeps on Severn side;
They cease not fighting, east and west,
On the marches of my breast.

Here the truceless armies yet
Trample, rolled in blood and sweat;
They kill and kill and never die;
And I think that each is I.

None will part us, none undo
The knot that makes one flesh of two,
Sick with hatred, sick with pain,
Strangling—When shall we be slain?

When shall I be dead and rid
Of the wrong my father did?
How long, how long, till spade and hearse
Put to sleep my mother's curse?

29

THE LENT LILY

'Tis spring; come out to ramble
The hilly brakes around,
For under thorn and bramble
About the hollow ground
The primroses are found.

And there's the windflower chilly
With all the winds at play,
And there's the Lenten lily
That has not long to stay
And dies on Easter day.

And since till girls go maying
You find the primrose still,

And find the windflower playing
With every wind at will,
But not the daffodil,

Bring baskets now, and sally
Upon the spring's array,
And bear from hill and valley
The daffodil away
That dies on Easter day.

30

Others, I am not the first,
Have willed more mischief than they durst:
If in the breathless night I too
Shiver now, 'tis nothing new.
More than I, if truth were told,
Have stood and sweated hot and cold,
And through their reins in ice and fire
Fear contended with desire.

Agued once like me were they,
But I like them shall win my way
Lastly to the bed of mould
Where there's neither heat nor cold.
But from my grave across my brow
Plays no wind of healing now,
And fire and ice within me fight
Beneath the suffocating night.

31

On Wenlock Edge the wood's in trouble
His forest fleece the Wrekin heaves;
The gale, it plies the saplings double,
And thick on Severn snow the leaves.

'Twould blow like this through holt and hanger
When Uricon the city stood:
'Tis the old wind in the old anger,
But then it threshed another wood.

Then, 'twas before my time, the Roman
At yonder heaving hill would stare:
The blood that warms an English yeoman,
The thoughts that hurt him, they were there.

There, like the wind through woods in riot,
Through him the gale of life blew high;

The tree of man was never quiet:
Then 'twas the Roman, now 'tis I.

The gale, it plies the saplings double,
It blows so hard, 'twill soon be gone:
To-day the Roman and his trouble
Are ashes under Uricon.

32

From far, from eve and morning
And yon twelve-winded sky,
The stuff of life to knit me
Blew hither: here am I.

Now—for a breath I tarry
Nor yet disperse apart—
Take my hand quick and tell me,
What have you in your heart.

Speak now, and I will answer;
How shall I help you, say;
Ere to the wind's twelve quarters
I take my endless way.

33

If truth in hearts that perish
Could move the powers on high,
I think the love I bear you
Should make you not to die.
Sure, sure, if stedfast meaning,
If single thought could save,
The world might end to-morrow,
You should not see the grave.

This long and sure-set liking,
This boundless will to please,
—Oh, you should live for ever
If there were help in these.
But now, since all is idle,
To this lost heart be kind,
Ere to a town you journey
Where friends are ill to find.

34

THE NEW MISTRESS

'Oh, sick I am to see you, will you never let me be?
You may be good for something but you are not good
   for me.
Oh, go where you are wanted, for you are not wanted
   here.'
And that was all the farewell when I parted from
   my dear.

'I will go where I am wanted, to a lady born and
   bred
Who will dress me free for nothing in a uniform
   of red;
She will not be sick to see me if I only keep it
   clean:

I will go where I am wanted for a soldier of the
  Queen.

'I will go where I am wanted, for the sergeant
  does not mind;
He may be sick to see me but he treats me very
  kind:
He gives me beer and breakfast and a ribbon for
  my cap,
And I never knew a sweetheart spend her money
  on a chap.

'I will go where I am wanted, where there's room
  for one or two,
And the men are none too many for the work
  there is to do;
Where the standing line wears thinner and the
  dropping dead lie thick;
And the enemies of England they shall see me
  and be sick.'

35

On the idle hill of summer,
Sleepy with the flow of streams,
Far I hear the steady drummer
Drumming like a noise in dreams.
Far and near and low and louder
On the roads of earth go by,
Dear to friends and food for powder,
Soldiers marching, all to die.

East and west on fields forgotten
Bleach the bones of comrades slain,
Lovely lads and dead and rotten;
None that go return again.
Far the calling bugles hollo,
High the screaming fife replies,
Gay the files of scarlet follow:
Woman bore me, I will rise.

36

White in the moon the long road lies,
The moon stands blank above;
White in the moon the long road lies
That leads me from my love.
Still hangs the hedge without a gust,
Still, still the shadows stay:
My feet upon the moonlit dust
Pursue the ceaseless way.

The world is round, so travellers tell,
And straight though reach the track,
Trudge on, trudge on, 'twill all be well,
The way will guide one back.
But ere the circle homeward hies
Far, far must it remove:
White in the moon the long road lies
That leads me from my love.

As through the wild green hills of Wyre
The train ran, changing sky and shire,
And far behind, a fading crest,
Low in the forsaken west
Sank the high-reared head of Clee,
My hand lay empty on my knee.
Aching on my knee it lay:
That morning half a shire away
So many an honest fellow's fist
Had wellnigh wrung it from the wrist.
Hand, said I, since now we part
From fields and men we know by heart,
For strangers' faces, strangers' lands,—
Hand, you have held true fellows' hands.

Be clean then; rot before you do
A thing they'd not believe of you.
You and I must keep from shame
In London streets the Shropshire name;
On banks of Thames they must not say
Severn breeds worse men than they;
And friends abroad must bear in mind
Friends at home they leave behind.
Oh, I shall be stiff and cold
When I forget you, hearts of gold;
The land where I shall mind you not
Is the land where all's forgot.
And if my foot returns no more
To Teme nor Corve nor Severn shore,
Luck, my lads, be with you still
By falling stream and standing hill,
By chiming tower and whispering tree,
Men that made a man of me.
About your work in town and farm
Still you'll keep my head from harm,
Still you'll help me, hands that gave
A grasp to friend me to the grave.

The winds out of the west land blow,
My friends have breathed them there;
Warm with the blood of lads I know
Comes east the sighing air.

It fanned their temples, filled their lungs,
Scattered their forelocks free;
My friends made words of it with tongues
That talk no more to me.

Their voices, dying as they fly,
Loose on the wind are sown;
The names of men blow soundless by,
My fellows' and my own.

Oh lads, at home I heard you plain,
But here your speech is still,

And down the sighing wind in vain
You hollo from the hill.

The wind and I, we both were there,
But neither long abode;
Now through the friendless world we fare
And sigh upon the road.

39

'Tis time, I think, by Wenlock town
The golden broom should blow;
The hawthorn sprinkled up and down
Should charge the land with snow.

Spring will not wait the loiterer's time
Who keeps so long away;
So others wear the broom and climb
The hedgerows heaped with may.

Oh tarnish late on Wenlock Edge,
Gold that I never see;
Lie long, high snowdrifts in the hedge
That will not shower on me.

40

Into my heart an air that kills
From yon far country blows:
What are those blue remembered hills,
What spires, what farms are those?

That is the land of lost content,
I see it shining plain,
The happy highways where I went
And cannot come again.

41

In my own shire, if I was sad,
Homely comforters I had:
The earth, because my heart was sore,
Sorrowed for the son she bore;
And standing hills, long to remain,
Shared their short-lived comrade's pain.
And bound for the same bourn as I,
On every road I wandered by,
Trod beside me, close and dear,
The beautiful and death-struck year:
Whether in the woodland brown

I heard the beechnut rustle down,
And saw the purple crocus pale
Flower about the autumn dale;
Or littering far the fields of May
Lady-smocks, a-bleaching lay
And like a skylit water stood
The bluebells in the azured wood.

Yonder, lightening other loads,
The seasons range the country roads,
But here in London streets I ken
No such helpmates, only men;
And these are not in plight to bear,
If they would, another's care.
They have enough as 'tis: I see
In many an eye that measures me
The mortal sickness of a mind
Too unhappy to be kind.
Undone with misery, all they can
Is to hate their fellow man;
And till they drop they needs must still
Look at you and wish you ill.

42

THE MERRY GUIDE

Once in the wind of morning
I ranged the thymy wold;
The world-wide air was azure
And all the brooks ran gold.

There through the dews beside me
Behold a youth that trod,
With feather cap on forehead,
And poised a golden rod.

With mien to match the morning
And gay delightful guise
And friendly brows and laughter
He looked me in the eyes.

Oh whence, I asked, and whither?
He smiled and would not say,
And looked at me and beckoned
And laughed and led the way.

And with kind looks and laughter
And nought to say beside
We two went on together,
I and my happy guide.

Across the glittering pastures
And empty upland still
And solitude of shepherds
High in the folded hill,

By hanging woods and hamlets
That gaze through orchards down
On many a windmill turning
And far-discovered town,

With gay regards of promise
And sure unslackened stride

And smiles and nothing spoken
Led on my merry guide.

By blowing realms of woodland
With sunstruck vanes afield
And cloud-led shadows sailing
About the windy weald.

By valley-guarded granges
And silver waters wide,
Content at heart I followed
With my delightful guide.

And like the cloudy shadows
Across the country blown
We two fare on for ever,
But not we two alone.

With the great gale we journey
That breathes from gardens thinned,
Borne in the drift of blossoms
Whose petals throng the wind;

Buoyed on the heaven–heard whisper
Of dancing leaflets whirled
From all the woods that autumn
Bereaves in all the world.

And midst the fluttering legion
Of all that ever died
I follow, and before us
Goes the delightful guide,

With lips that brim with laughter
But never once respond,
And feet that fly on feathers,
And serpent–circled wand.

43

THE IMMORTAL PART

When I meet the morning beam,
Or lay me down at night to dream,
I hear my bones within me say,
'Another night, another day.

'When shall this slough of sense be cast,
This dust of thoughts be laid at last,
The man of flesh and soul be slain
And the man of bone remain?

'This tongue that talks, these lungs that shout,
These thews that hustle us about,
This brain that fills the skull with schemes,
And its humming hive of dreams,—

'These to-day are proud in power
And lord it in their little hour:
The immortal bones obey control
Of dying flesh and dying soul.

''Tis long till eve and morn are gone:
Slow the endless night comes on,
And late to fulness grows the birth
That shall last as long as earth.

'Wanderers eastward, wanderers west,
Know you why you cannot rest?
'Tis that every mother's son
Travails with a skeleton.

Lie down in the bed of dust;
Bear the fruit that bear you must;
Bring the eternal seed to light,
And morn is all the same as night.

'Rest you so from trouble sore,
Fear the heat o' the sun no more,

Nor the snowing winter wild,
Now you labour not with child.

'Empty vessel, garment cast,
We that wore you long shall last.
—Another night, another day.'
So my bones within me say.

Therefore they shall do my will
To-day while I am master still,
And flesh and soul, now both are strong,
Shall hale the sullen slaves along,

Before this fire of sense decay,
This smoke of thought blow clean away,
And leave with ancient night alone
The stedfast and enduring bone.

44

Shot? so quick, so clean an ending?
Oh that was right, lad, that was brave:
Yours was not an ill for mending,
'Twas best to take it to the grave.

Oh you had forethought, you could reason,
And saw your road and where it led,
And early wise and brave in season
Put the pistol to your head.

Oh soon, and better so than later
After long disgrace and scorn,
You shot dead the household traitor,
The soul that should not have been born.

Right you guessed the rising morrow
And scorned to tread the mire you must:
Dust's your wages, son of sorrow,
But men may come to worse than dust.

Souls undone, undoing others,—
Long time since the tale began.
You would not live to wrong your brothers:
Oh lad, you died as fits a man.

Now to your grave shall friend and stranger
With ruth and some with envy come:
Undishonoured, clear of danger,
Clean of guilt, pass hence and home.

Turn safe to rest, no dreams, no waking;
And here, man, here's the wreath I've made:
'Tis not a gift that's worth the taking,
But wear it and it will not fade.

45

If it chance your eye offend you,
Pluck it out, lad, and be sound:
'Twill hurt, but here are salves to friend you,
And many a balsam grows on ground.

And if your hand or foot offend you,
Cut it off, lad, and be whole;
But play the man, stand up and end you,
When your sickness is your soul.

46

Bring, in this timeless grave to throw,
No cypress, sombre on the snow;
Snap not from the bitter yew
His leaves that live December through;
Break no rosemary, bright with rime
And sparkling to the cruel clime;
Nor plod the winter land to look
For willows in the icy brook
To cast them leafless round him: bring
No spray that ever buds in spring.

But if the Christmas field has kept
Awns the last gleaner overstept,
Or shrivelled flax, whose flower is blue
A single season, never two;
Or if one haulm whose year is o'er

Shivers on the upland frore,
—Oh, bring from hill and stream and plain
Whatever will not flower again,
To give him comfort: he and those
Shall bide eternal bedfellows
Where low upon the couch he lies
Whence he never shall arise.

47

THE CARPENTER'S SON

'Here the hangman stops his cart:
Now the best of friends must part.
Fare you well, for ill fare I:
Live, lads, and I will die.

'Oh, at home had I but stayed
'Prenticed to my father's trade,
Had I stuck to plane and adze,
I had not been lost, my lads.

'Then I might have built perhaps
Gallows-trees for other chaps,
Never dangled on my own,
Had I but left ill alone.

'Now, you see, they hang me high,
And the people passing by
Stop to shake their fists and curse;
So 'tis come from ill to worse.

'Here hang I, and right and left
Two poor fellows hang for theft:
All the same's the luck we prove,
Though the midmost hangs for love.

'Comrades all, that stand and gaze,
Walk henceforth in other ways;
See my neck and save your own:
Comrades all, leave ill alone.

'Make some day a decent end,
Shrewder fellows than your friend.
Fare you well, for ill fare I:
Live, lads, and I will die.'

48

Be still, my soul, be still; the arms you bear are
   brittle,
Earth and high heaven are fixt of old and founded
   strong.
Think rather,—call to thought, if now you grieve
   a little,
The days when we had rest, O soul, for they were
   long.

Men loved unkindness then, but lightless in the
   quarry
I slept and saw not; tears fell down, I did not
   mourn;
Sweat ran and blood sprang out and I was never
   sorry:
Then it was well with me, in days ere I was born.

Now, and I muse for why and never find the
　　reason,
I pace the earth, and drink the air, and feel the
　　sun.
Be still, be still, my soul; it is but for a season:
Let us endure an hour and see injustice done.

Ay, look: high heaven and earth ail from the
　　prime foundation;
All thoughts to rive the heart are here, and all are
　　vain:
Horror and scorn and hate and fear and indig-
　　nation—
Oh why did I awake? when shall I sleep again?

49

Think no more, lad; laugh, be jolly:
Why should men make haste to die?
Empty heads and tongues a-talking
Make the rough road easy walking,
And the feather pate of folly
Bears the falling sky.

Oh, 'tis jesting, dancing, drinking
Spins the heavy world around.
If young hearts were not so clever,
Oh, they would be young for ever:
Think no more; 'tis only thinking
Lays lads underground.

50

Clunton and Clunbury,
Clungunford and Clun,
Are the quietest places
Under the sun.

In valleys of springs of rivers,
By Ony and Teme and Clun,
The country for easy livers,
The quietest under the sun,

We still had sorrows to lighten,
One could not be always glad,
And lads knew trouble at Knighton
When I was a Knighton lad.

By bridges that Thames runs under,
In London, the town built ill,
'Tis sure small matter for wonder
If sorrow is with one still.

And if as a lad grows older
The troubles he bears are more,
He carries his griefs on a shoulder
That handselled them long before.

Where shall one halt to deliver
This luggage I'd lief set down?
Not Thames, not Teme is the river,
Nor London nor Knighton the town:

'Tis a long way further than Knighton,
A quieter place than Clun,
Where doomsday may thunder and lighten
And little 'twill matter to one.

51

Loitering with a vacant eye
Along the Grecian gallery,
And brooding on my heavy ill,
I met a statue standing still.
Still in marble stone stood he,
And stedfastly he looked at me.
'Well met,' I thought the look would say,
'We both were fashioned far away;
We neither knew when we were young,
These Londoners we live among.'

Still he stood and eyed me hard,
An earnest and a grave regard:
'What, lad, drooping with your lot?
I too would be where I am not.

I too survey that endless line
Of men whose thoughts are not as mine.
Years, ere you stood up from rest,
On my neck the collar prest;
Years, when you lay down your ill,
I shall stand and bear it still.
Courage, lad, 'tis not for long:
Stand, quit you like stone, be strong.'
So I thought his look would say;
And light on me my trouble lay,
And I stept out in flesh and bone
Manful like the man of stone.

52

Far in a western brookland
That bred me long ago
The poplars stand and tremble
By pools I used to know.
There, in the windless night-time,
The wanderer, marvelling why,
Halts on the bridge to hearken
How soft the poplars sigh.
He hears: no more remembered
In fields where I was known,
Here I lie down in London
And turn to rest alone.
There, by the starlit fences,
The wanderer halts and hears
My soul that lingers sighing
About the glimmering weirs.

53

THE TRUE LOVER

The lad came to the door at night,
When lovers crown their vows,
And whistled soft and out of sight
In shadow of the boughs.

'I shall not vex you with my face
Henceforth, my love, for aye;
So take me in your arms a space
Before the east is grey.

'When I from hence away am past
I shall not find a bride,
And you shall be the first and last
I ever lay beside.'

She heard and went and knew not why;
Her heart to his she laid;
Light was the air beneath the sky
But dark under the shade.

'Oh do you breathe, lad, that your breast
Seems not to rise and fall,
And here upon my bosom prest
There beats no heart at all?'

'Oh loud, my girl, it once would knock,
You should have felt it then;
But since for you I stopped the clock
It never goes again.'

'Oh lad, what is it, lad, that drips
Wet from your neck on mine?
What is it falling on my lips,
My lad, that tastes of brine?'

'Oh like enough 'tis blood, my dear,
For when the knife has slit
The throat across from ear to ear
'Twill bleed because of it.'

Under the stars the air was light
But dark below the boughs,
The still air of the speechless night,
When lovers crown their vows.

54

With rue my heart is laden
For golden friends I had,
For many a rose-lipt maiden
And many a lightfoot lad.

By brooks too broad for leaping
The lightfoot boys are laid;
The rose-lipt girls are sleeping
In fields where roses fade.

55

Westward on the high-hilled plains
Where for me the world began,
Still, I think, in newer veins
Frets the changeless blood of man.
Now that other lads than I
Strip to bathe on Severn shore,
They, no help, for all they try,
Tread the mill I trod before.

There, when hueless is the west
And the darkness hushes wide,
Where the lad lies down to rest
Stands the troubled dream beside.
There, on thoughts that once were mine,
Day looks down the eastern steep,
And the youth at morning shine
Makes the vow he will not keep.

56

THE DAY OF BATTLE

'Far I hear the bugle blow
To call me where I would not go,
And the guns begin the song,
"Soldier, fly or stay for long."

'Comrade, if to turn and fly
Made a soldier never die,
Fly I would, for who would not?
'Tis sure no pleasure to be shot.

'But since the man that runs away
Lives to die another day,
And cowards' funerals, when they come,
Are not wept so well at home,

'Therefore, though the best is bad,
Stand and do the best, my lad;
Stand and fight and see your slain,
And take the bullet in your brain.'

57

You smile upon your friend to-day,
To-day his ills are over;
You hearken to the lover's say,
And happy is the lover.

'Tis late to hearken, late to smile,
But better late than never:
I shall have lived a little while
Before I die for ever.

58

When I came last to Ludlow
  Amidst the moonlight pale,
Two friends kept step beside me,
  Two honest lads and hale.

Now Dick lies long in the churchyard,
  And Ned lies long in jail,
And I come home to Ludlow
  Amidst the moonlight pale.

THE ISLE OF PORTLAND

The star-filled seas are smooth to-night
From France to England strown;
Black towers above the Portland light
The felon-quarried stone.

On yonder island, not to rise,
Never to stir forth free,
Far from his folk a dead lad lies
That once was friends with me.

Lie you easy, dream you light,
And sleep you fast for aye;
And luckier may you find the night
Than ever you found the day.

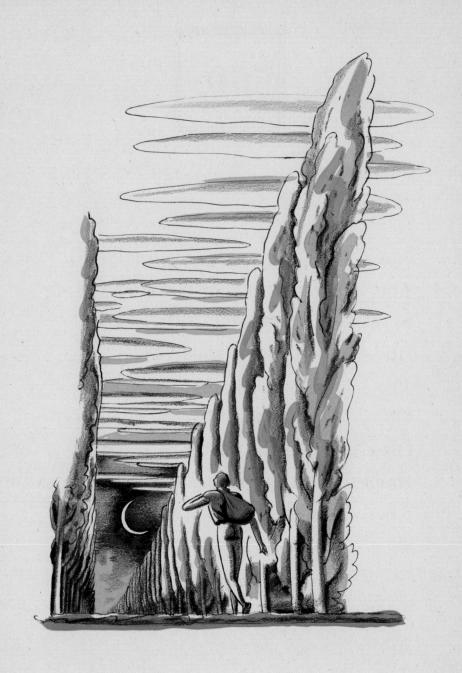

60

Now hollow fires burn out to black,
And lights are guttering low:
Square your shoulders, lift your pack,
And leave your friends and go.

Oh never fear, man, nought's to dread,
Look not left nor right:
In all the endless road you tread
There's nothing but the night.

HUGHLEY STEEPLE

The vane on Hughley steeple
Veers bright, a far-known sign,
And there lie Hughley people,
And there lie friends of mine.
Tall in their midst the tower
Divides the shade and sun,
And the clock strikes the hour
And tells the time to none.

To south the headstones cluster,
The sunny mounds lie thick;
The dead are more in muster
At Hughley than the quick.
North for a soon-told number,

Chill graves the sexton delves,
And steeple-shadowed slumber
The slayers of themselves.

To north, to south, lie parted,
With Hughley tower above,
The kind, the single-hearted,
The lads I used to love.
And, south or north, 'tis only
A choice of friends one knows,
And I shall ne'er be lonely
Asleep with these or those.

62

'Terence, this is stupid stuff:
You eat your victuals fast enough;
There can't be much amiss, 'tis clear,
To see the rate you drink your beer.
But oh, good Lord, the verse you make,
It gives a chap the belly-ache.
The cow, the old cow, she is dead;
It sleeps well, the horned head:
We poor lads, 'tis our turn now
To hear such tunes as killed the cow.
Pretty friendship 'tis to rhyme
Your friends to death before their time
Moping melancholy mad:
Come, pipe a tune to dance to, lad.'

Why, if 'tis dancing you would be,
There's brisker pipes than poetry.
Say, for what were hop-yards meant,
Or why was Burton built on Trent?
Oh many a peer of England brews
Livelier liquor than the Muse,
And malt does more than Milton can
To justify God's ways to man.
Ale, man, ale's the stuff to drink
For fellows whom it hurts to think:
Look into the pewter pot
To see the world as the world's not.
And faith, 'tis pleasant till 'tis past:
The mischief is that 'twill not last.
Oh I have been to Ludlow fair
And left my necktie God knows where,
And carried half way home, or near,
Pints and quarts of Ludlow beer:
Then the world seemed none so bad,
And I myself a sterling lad;
And down in lovely muck I've lain,
Happy till I woke again.

Then I saw the morning sky:
Heigho, the tale was all a lie;
The world, it was the old world yet,
I was I, my things were wet,
And nothing now remained to do
But begin the game anew.
Therefore, since the world has still
Much good, but much less good than ill,
And while the sun and moon endure
Luck's a chance, but trouble's sure,
I'd face it as a wise man would,
And train for ill and not for good.
'Tis true, the stuff I bring for sale
Is not so brisk a brew as ale:
Out of a stem that scored the hand
I wrung it in a weary land.
But take it: if the smack is sour,
The better for the embittered hour;
It should do good to heart and head
When your soul is in my soul's stead;
And I will friend you, if I may
In the dark and cloudy day.

There was a king reigned in the East:
There, when kings will sit to feast,
They get their fill before they think
With poisoned meat and poisoned drink.
He gathered all that springs to birth
From the many-venomed earth;
First a little, thence to more,
He sampled all her killing store;
And easy, smiling, seasoned sound,
Sate the king when healths went round.
They put arsenic in his meat
And stared aghast to watch him eat;
They poured strychnine in his cup
And shook to see him drink it up:
They shook, they stared as white's their shirt:
Them it was their poison hurt.
—I tell the tale that I heard told.
Mithridates, he died old.

63

I hoed and trenched and weeded,
And took the flowers to fair:
I brought them home unheeded;
The hue was not the wear.
So up and down I sow them
For lads like me to find,
When I shall lie below them,
A dead man out of mind.

Some seed the birds devour,
And some the season mars,
But here and there will flower
The solitary stars,
And fields will yearly bear them
As light-leaved spring comes on,
And luckless lads will wear them
When I am dead and gone.

APPENDIX:

I. History of the Poems

II. Notes on the Poems

III. A Critical Garland

COMPILED BY CARL J. WEBER FOR THE JUBILEE EDITION ISSUED

BY THE COLBY COLLEGE LIBRARY ON THE OCCASION OF

THE FIFTIETH ANNIVERSARY OF A SHROPSHIRE LAD

I. History of the Poems

In the closing weeks of 1895 a manuscript entitled "Poems by Terence Hearsay" was submitted to the London publishing house of Macmillan and Company. On the advice of their reader, John Morley, the Macmillans declined to publish the poems, and the author considered where to turn next. His friend Alfred W. Pollard, after suggesting a change in the title of the manuscript, introduced the poet to another publisher, Kegan Paul. The latter eventually agreed to publish the re-entitled work, provided the poet would pay for the printing. He would. Accordingly, five hundred copies of *A Shropshire Lad* by A. E. HOUSMAN were printed, and the book was published in February, 1896. A dozen copies were sent out to magazines and newspapers.

Of the five hundred copies of the first edition, one hundred and fifty were sent to the New York office of the John Lane Company for sale in the United States. One copy was bought in a Boston bookstore by an unknown American poet named Edwin Arlington Robinson, who promptly called it to the attention of his friend William Vaughn Moody. Another copy was bought by Louise Imogen Guiney, who wrote an ecstatic review of the book—the second to appear in the United States. Less than a dozen American reviews were scattered over more than a dozen months.

The fame of the poems spread slowly—very slowly. Shortly before *McClure's Magazine* began printing the poems, an unauthorized edition appeared in Philadelphia; and in the middle of the five-year period during which the lyrics were printed in *McClure's*, another American edition was published in Portland, Maine. Housman made no effort to stop them. "American publishers," he said, "have a perfect right to issue unauthorized copies." The result has been, eventually, a large number of American printings and the creation of an immense audience for Housman. When his English publisher came to the United States in 1922, he gained the impression that *A Shropshire Lad* would open any doors; and wherever he went, he found that the name of Housman was sufficient to ensure for him a welcome as the poet's publisher. By many an American reader *A Shropshire Lad* has come to be regarded as the most important book of poetry published in the last half-century.

When Kegan Paul in London signified that a second printing would have to be again at Housman's own expense, the poet accepted the offer of Mr. Grant Richards to publish the book without cost to Housman, and on September 14, 1898, Richards issued the second edition of five hundred copies of *A Shropshire Lad*. As in the case of the first edition, a dozen copies were sent out to magazines and newspapers, including some which had already reviewed the book in 1896.

Even with the help of this second dozen of British reviews of the book, it moved very slowly; and, according to Grant Richards, *A Shropshire Lad* succeeded much more quickly in America than in England. The English publisher thought that the printing of some of the poems in *McClure's Magazine*, which then had a huge and important circulation, had much to do with the quickness of this American appreciation.

Appreciation led to collection, and American libraries, public and private, have of late given increasing attention to A. E. Housman. The manuscript of *A Shropshire Lad* is now in the Library of Congress. On the fiftieth anniversary of the publication of the first edition, the Colby College Library opened a Jubilee Exhibition of copies of all the editions of the book which are now on its shelves. This Colby *Shropshire Lad* collection was assembled over a period of years by a friend of the Colby Library and presented to that library on the fiftieth anniversary, in concrete illustration of Samuel Johnson's prescription for the collecting of all the editions of an important book and presenting them to a library.

II. Notes on the Poems

A. E. Housman met his class in Horace as usual, one morning in May, 1914, and proceeded to dissect, with the wit and the sarcasm for which he was famous, the seventh ode in Book Four: "Diffugere nives," etc. Then he startled his students by saying that he would like to spend a few minutes "considering this ode simply as poetry." After reading it aloud with deep emotion, he stated, with obvious embarrassment at his own unaccustomed communicativeness: "*That I regard as the most beautiful poem in ancient literature.*" Whereupon he picked up his papers and walked quickly out of the classroom.

Housman's great admiration for the ode of Horace had not prevented its dissection by him, nor had his critical treatment of it decreased its power to move him.

A few years ago I heard a roomful of American college teachers, assembled in New York City, spend two hours discussing how to read one line in one of the poems in this book and what the poem meant. In the light of that experience I feel no call to apologize for the notes here presented: That Robin Hood among readers whose mind shoots with swift and unerring accuracy straight to the goal of the poet's meaning will know how to ignore all notes; but for the aid of puzzled professors of poetry, for the enlightenment of Americans unfamiliar with Shropshire, for the information of those who may be curious about the ways of the poet to whom the world has been for half a century indebted for this golden treasury, and for the help of all those readers who do not find that the emotional enjoyment of poetry is lessened by an intelligent grasp of its meaning, I offer the following notes.

1

In the year 1887 Queen Victoria's Golden Jubilee was the occasion for national celebrations in England. On Jubilee night a small company walked from Housman's home at Bromsgrove, Fockbury House, to the top of a hill nearby. In the Housman family this hill was known as Mount Pisgah. It stood in a field at the top of Worms Ash Lane, and Housman often went there to watch the sunset. Walking was his chief recreation, from the time the Housmans moved to Bromsgrove in 1873, and he took particular pleasure in reaching some spot from which he could see an extensive view. On Jubilee Night he and his companions climbed "Mount Pisgah" and there watched the bonfires burning, "right round the counties, from the Malvern Hills to the Wrekin, and farther."

Line 1. *Clee* is a hill in southern Shropshire.

19. *Nile*: during the eighteen-nineties when these poems were composed there was much fighting along the Nile in Egypt.

20. *Severn*: this river flows through Shropshire.

28. *the Fifty-third*: the Shropshire Regiment of Infantry. These "lads" were not all creatures of Housman's imagination. His brother Herbert, to whom he was strongly attached, was a soldier. Herbert Housman was the only one of five brothers who showed no inclination for a life of study, and when he was twenty-one he enlisted in the Queen's Royal Rifles. He was killed in action in 1901. The poet's affection for his brother made it impossible for him to write the last line of this poem in the spirit of bitter sarcasm which Frank Harris "in all sincerity" found there. Harris once told Kipling that he mixed his patriotism with snobbery, but to Housman Harris said: "You have poked fun at the whole thing and made splendid mockery of it." Housman replied sharply: "I never intended to poke fun, as you call it, at patriotism, and I can find nothing in the sentiment to make

mockery of. I meant it sincerely. If Englishmen breed as good men as their fathers, then God will save their Queen. I can only reject and resent your—your truculent praise."

I have examined twenty-five American anthologies covering the poetry of Housman's period, in the thought that editorial selections among the *Shropshire* poems might give some indication of their popularity with American readers. This first poem appears in three of these anthologies.

2

"Loveliest of trees" is printed in thirteen of the twenty-five anthologies. It appeared under the title "Song" in *McClure's Magazine* for April, 1905.

3

No anthology has reprinted this poem. It was composed in January, 1895. It and other poems in this book also dealing with soldiers led one of the directors of the firm that first published the volume to propose to Housman that he "make the whole affair into a romance of enlistment." He suggested "a design on the cover representing a yokel in a smock frock with a bunch of recruiting-sergeant's ribbons in his hat." Housman wisely rejected the suggestion.

4

This poem has been very popular with American editors. It appears in eighteen out of twenty-five anthologies.

8. *Straws*: is strewn across.

14. *Forelands*: headlands or capes.

18. *pallets*: small beds.

5

1. *goldcup*: marigold.

3. *to tell the hours*: by the number of seeds that fly away when children blow on the dandelion.

6

Reprinted in only one anthology.

7

Geoffrey Tillotson has called the stanza used in this poem "one of the most notable forms" in the book, and he has been unable to find any earlier example of it. Ernest Dowson's *Verses*, also published in 1896, uses virtually the same stanza.

1. *Ludlow*: a large town in southern Shropshire.

9. *trampling*: the word "tramping" which appears in the Illustrated Edition Company's book (1932, p.24), in both formats, and in the half dozen derivative publications (De Luxe, Three Sirens, Grosset, Arden, Concord, and Cleveland) is of course a misprint.

8

This poem was composed in August, 1894. "It . . . seemed, when one first read 'Farewell to barn and stack and tree,' that never again could a man render so perfectly the atmosphere of mortal tragedy."—William Rose Benét, 1923.

3. *Terence*: see note to 62.

19. *Lammastide*: the first day of August, formerly celebrated in England as a harvest festival.

21. *rick*: a stack of hay or straw.

9. *Shrewsbury*: the county-seat of Shropshire.

10

9. *The boys*: Housman's sister has assured readers that it is a mistake to try to identify him personally with the boys of Shropshire. He was a Worcestershire lad.

11

Reprinted in only one anthology.

12

This poem appears in three anthologies.

13

The first draft of this poem was composed in January, 1895. It was printed in *McClure's* in May 1906, in *Current Literature* in December 1907, and it appears in eleven American anthologies.

3. *crowns . . . guineas*: British coins. A crown is worth about a dollar; a guinea about five dollars.

14

6. *sound*: fathom.

10. *Beneath the blue of day*: this was an eleventh-hour emendation of the manuscript reading, "From Thulë to Cathay."

13. *sain*: protect, originally by making the sign of the cross.

15

Printed under the title "Verses" in *McClure's Magazine* for March 1908.

16

In no anthology.

17

In only one out of twenty-five anthologies.

18

Composed in May 1895. Printed in *McClure's*, January 1905; in seven anthologies.

19

"The poem by which the world will longest remember Alfred Housman."—James Brannin, 1925.

"One of my favorites."—Thomas Hardy.

Reprinted in thirteen American anthologies.

2. *chaired*: carried on a chair.

14. *cut*: broken.

17. *rout*: a throng or crowd.

20

In the June 1904 *McClure's* this poem was entitled "Wishing." In one anthology it is called "A Look into Water."

11. *cressy*: Housman's manuscript read "rushy" until he made a "tenth-hour" emendation.

21

Composed in July 1891; reprinted in seven American anthologies.

1. *Bredon*: a high hill in Worcestershire, near the Gloucestershire border. Housman explained: "That poem was written early, before I knew the book would be a Shropshire book."

3. *both the shires*: Worcestershire and Gloucestershire.

8. *coloured*: Housman's brother Laurence once asked him if his "so happily-chosen adjectives had come to him spontaneously or after labor and with difficulty," and he cited "coloured counties" as an instance. The poet replied: "When I wrote the poem I put down . . . a quite ordinary adjective, which didn't satisfy me; others followed. Then . . . I went to bed and dreamed, and in my dream I hit on the word 'painted.' When I woke up, I saw that 'painted' wouldn't do, but it gave me 'coloured' as the right word." In the first draft of the poem which Laurence Housman found in his brother's note-book, the alternative adjectives ran: sunny, pleasant, checkered, patterned.

8. *counties*: in addition to the two named in the note to line 3 above, Herefordshire, Warwickshire, and Oxfordshire can be seen from Bredon Hill.

17. *thyme*: a mint plant.

22

Entitled "Saluto!" in *McClure's* in October 1906.

23

An amusing parody of this poem was written by Gerald Gould.

15. *mintage*: this line in the first draft of the poem read: "They carry unspoilt into safety the honor of man." Laurence Housman remarks: "Surely in that change one sees in a flash inspiration at work."

24

In four anthologies.

25

In only two American anthologies.

26

Composed in June (1895?).

27

"I could not say that I have a favourite among my poems. Thomas Hardy's was No. XXVII. . . . Mrs. Hardy told me his opinion."—A. E. H., 1933, 1935.

This poem appears in nine out of twenty-five American anthologies.

28

Composed in January 1895. The Welsh Marches are the borderlands between England and Wales, long the scene of fighting between the English and the Welsh. The word is *not* "marshes."

13. *Buildwas*: an early town where there are the ruins of a Norman abbey church.

Lines 13 and 14 have "a grandeur and muffled music which Milton might have owned."—Louise Imogen Guiney, 1897.

16. *got*: begot.

29

Composed in April 1895.

30

In no anthology.

31

First draft composed November 1895. This poem, says Louise Imogen Guiney, "with its sympathetic sense of things bygone, of the tingling human past which lies about no yokel's dreams, could only have come from a hand subdued, and manners and a mind long mellowed."

1. *Wenlock Edge*: hills in southeastern Shropshire.

2. *Wrekin*: "some of my topographical details are wrong and imaginary. The Wrekin is wooded, and Wenlock Edge along the western side, but the Clees and most of the other hills are grass or heather."—A. E. H.

3. *plies*: bends.

5. *hanger*: a wood on the slope of a hill.

6. *Uricon*: one of the chief Roman cities in ancient Britain, in what is now southeastern Shropshire.

32

2. *twelve-winded*: there are twelve "quarters" (line 11) from which the wind can be described as coming.

33

In only one anthology.

34 AND 35

In two anthologies.

36

Twice printed in *McClure's*: in October 1904 under the title "The World is Round" (line 9); in March 1906 under the title "Song."

37

18. *the Shropshire name*: "I was not born in Shropshire at all, but in Worcestershire. The Shropshire hills were our western horizon, and hence my sentiment for the county, I suppose."—A. E. H.

38

10. *Loose*: in all editions until 1922 the word here was "Thick."

39

Composed in February 1893.

40

This poem, more than any other, sums up Housman's pangs of remembrance in London of his home in Bromsgrove and his boyhood there.

41

Housman's sister has stated that, in some of the poems, "he throws off the figment of a Shropshire lad and refers unmistakably to his own home and boyhood" in Worcestershire. This is one of them.

42

One of the earliest: composed in September 1890.

2. *wold*: stretch of open, uncultivated ground.

6. *youth*: Mercury (or Hermes), who was commonly represented as wearing a cap with wings (line 7), as having wingéd sandals (line 59), and as bearing a golden staff (line 8) encircled with serpents (line 60).

20. *guide*: Hermes was appointed by the gods to conduct the souls of the dead from the upper to the lower world.

24. *folded*: having a sheepfold.

33–36. *By blowing . . . weald*: in Housman's first draft this stanza read:

> By windy shires of woodland
>   With steeples dim-revealed,
> And cloudy shadows racing
>   On all the endless weald.

Laurence Housman remarks: "There is improvement in every line and in every change of word."

36. *weald*: practically the same as "wold" (line 2).

37. *granges*: barns.

43

Reprinted in three anthologies.

44

9–10. *better . . . than . . . long disgrace*: this poem was suggested to Housman by the suicide on August 6, 1895, of an eighteen-year-old Woolwich Cadet. The young man left a letter addressed to the coroner, explaining why he had taken his own life. The poem here almost quotes the cadet's letter: "I am putting an end to my life after . . . careful deliberation. . . . I will state the main reasons which have determined me. The first is utter cowardice and despair. There is only one thing in this world which would make me thoroughly happy; that one thing I have no earthly hope of obtaining. The second . . . is that I have absolutely ruined my own life; but I thank God that as yet . . . I have not morally injured . . . anyone else. Now I am quite certain that I could not live another five years without doing so, and for that reason alone, even if the first did not exist, I should do what I am doing. . . . At all events it is . . . better than a long series of . . . disgraces."

45

1. *eye offend*: "If thine eye offend thee, pluck it out."— *Mark*, 9:47.

5. *hand or foot*: "If thy hand offend thee, cut it off. . . . And if thy foot offend thee, cut it off."— *Mark*, 9:43–45.

7. *stand up and end you*: an amusing and caustic parody of this theme and meter was written by Hugh Kingsmill:

"What, still alive at twenty-two,
A clean, upstanding chap like you . . . ."

Housman spoke of this parody as "the best he had seen."

46

In only one American anthology.

47

Composed in August 1895.

48

"Bitter but magnificent stanzas."—Louise Imogen Guiney.

14. *rive*: this word was arrived at by way of no fewer than eight alternatives: vex, plague, tear, wrench, rend, wring, break, and pierce. "Most of the finest of his poems came with most difficulty."—Laurence Housman.

49

In nine American anthologies.

50

The four villages mentioned in the introductory stanza are in southwestern Shropshire. "The stanza is traditional." —A. E. H.

2. *Ony . . . Clun*: rivers.

7. *Knighton*: a town on the river Teme.

8. *Knighton lad*: Did this line originally read: "When I was a Shropshire lad"? Alfred W. Pollard, whom Housman asked to arrange for the publication of these poems, suggested that the poet had not given them an attractive title (see note to 62) "and that in the phrase 'a Shropshire lad' which he had used in the poem, he had much a better one. He agreed at once, and I think the change helped." It certainly did.

16. *handselled*: had a foretaste of.

51

"Glimpses of the heart-sickness suffered by A. E. H. in London when he went there to live in 1882 are found in his poems. The whole of *A Shropshire Lad* was written while he was there. In some of the poems . . . he . . . refers unmistakably to his own home and boyhood . . . as . . . in No. 51." —Housman's sister Katharine.

52

Composed in 1891–1892. The poem refers to his own boyhood in Bromsgrove.

9. *no more remembered*: in 1922 Housman changed to this phrase the earlier reading of the line: "long since forgotten."

The poem was the first of fifteen printings of *Shropshire Lad* poems in *McClure's Magazine*. It appeared in December 1903 under the title "Song." It has been reprinted in eight American anthologies.

53

The first draft of this poem was composed in December 1894.

54

Composed in August 1893. Printed in *McClure's*, January 1906, and in sixteen out of twenty-five anthologies.

55

In only two anthologies.

56

Composed in March 1895.

4. *soldier*: written with thoughts of his brother Herbert. See note on I, 28.

57

Printed under the title "I shall have lived" (from line 7) in *McClure's* for March 1905.

58

Composed in July 1895.

59 AND 60

In only one anthology.

61

1–2. *vane* : : : *far-known sign*: Hughley is a village in Shropshire, but its steeple is borrowed from another church, which is actually "buried away in a valley." Housman's explanation was that the place he really meant had an ugly name, so he borrowed the name Hughley, because he felt that he "could not invent another name that sounded so nice. . . . I thought of putting a note to say that Hughley was only a name, but then I thought that would merely disturb the reader. I did not apprehend that the faithful would be making pilgrimages to these holy places."—A. E. H., 1896.

12. *quick*: living.

62

1. *Terence*: Housman's original title for this book was *The Poems of Terence Hearsay*. A. W. Pollard suggested that this was not an attractive title and proposed the one by which the book is now known. In the opening fourteen lines of this poem, Housman imagines one of his listeners replying to him.

18. *Burton*: a city in Staffordshire, famous for its breweries.

21–22. *malt . . . to man*: these oft-quoted words were inscribed on a loving-cup given to Housman by his students at University College, London, on his appointment to the professorship at Cambridge University. The lettering was a little hard to read, and when Housman showed the cup to his brother Laurence, the latter asked: "Is this Latin?" "No," replied the poet, "English, very good English."

46. *Luck's a chance*: the manuscript read "Good's—". "Luck" was an eleventh-hour change.

51. *scored*: cut.

75. *the tale*: from Pliny's *Natural History*.

76. *Mithridates*: greatest of Kings of Pontus, 122–64 B.C. This poem appears in eight American anthologies.

63

2. *flowers*: i.e., these poems.

4. *wear*: fashion.

8. *out of mind*: forgotten.

Two of the stanzas of this poem came into the poet's head during an afternoon walk, a third came with a little coaxing, but the fourth was a laborious business. "I wrote it thirteen times," Housman said, "and it was more than a twelvemonth before I got it right." He would never tell which was which.

III. A Critical Garland

The day when I first opened *A Shropshire Lad* and found there more than thirty very good poems awaiting me, was one of the great events of my life. Alfred had kept it a sealed secret from his family until the day of publication.

LAURENCE HOUSMAN

A Shropshire Lad brought no attention to the author, who did not even take the trouble to secure copyright in his work. But year by year this group of short lyrics has risen in critical esteem.

STITH THOMPSON

Not since the Elizabethans have there been lyrics so delicate and yet so firm, so seemingly casual yet so inevitable. They seem part of the permanent literature of the English language. Many of them are as nearly perfect as lyrics can hope to be.

LOUIS UNTERMEYER

The songs published under the title *A Shropshire Lad* are, I think, as likely to be read and cherished two hundred years from now as anything written in the English language during the past half-century. . . . *A Shropshire Lad* went far and found a home in many hearts. In the most unexpected corner of the English-speaking world you would find men who could say its every line to themselves as they walked alone down country lanes far, far from Shropshire. . . . Housman wrote more of what is poetry to me than anyone now living.

ALEXANDER WOOLLCOTT

In 1922 I read the terse note by Housman in his *Last Poems* on the "continuous excitement" in which he wrote *A Shropshire Lad* during the early months of 1895. . . . Most of the Shropshire lyrics . . . I knew by heart.

CARL VAN DOREN

His regard for *A Shropshire Lad* was like that of a mother for her first-born. Over and over again he showed a special, a tender, affection for it. He believed its lyrics were a higher quality than those of *Last Poems*. He was adamant against every proposition to bind the two volumes in one. He wished it presented and offered to the reader as a whole, and alone.   PERCY WITHERS

There seems to me to be no question as to the enduring quality of A. E. Housman's poetry. I do not think of any living writer whose work is likely to live longer, if as long.
                    EDWIN ARLINGTON ROBINSON

Viola Roseboro, chief reader on *McClure's Magazine* when I went there in 1902, first introduced A. E. Housman's work to me. Soon after, Mr. McClure appointed me poetry editor of the magazine and agreed to the unusual procedure of printing in its pages, with Housman's permission, poems from a book already published. In this manner I was responsible for introducing the poet to America, in as much as his book at that time was practically unheard of. For years and years the little Lane edition went everywhere with me in my pocket and was read aloud not only to friends like Van Wyck Brooks but later, when I took up the lecture platform, to audiences all over the United States. *A Shropshire Lad* still seems to me the supreme book it seemed in my youth and surer of survival than any other poetry written in my time. It is all the great machinery of Greek purgation gathered into a dewdrop.   WITTER BYNNER

I read *A Shropshire Lad*, always with tears. There is not much else than tears in them, but they are perfect of their kind.   GEORGE SANTAYANA

It is long since we have caught just this note in English verse—the note of intense feeling uttering itself in language of unadorned precision, uncontorted truth.
                              WILLIAM ARCHER

The charm of such simple lyric or ballad verse as we find here is hard to convey. . . . It would be difficult to over-praise the exquisite simplicity of these verses.

RICHARD LE GALLIENNE

Housman kept the letter of an American who had looked after a wounded British soldier in France and wrote to tell Housman about it. One day the American took *A Shropshire Lad* to the wounded man. The man smiled and took from under his pillow a copy of his own, all tattered, torn and blood-stained. It had been in his pocket throughout the War of 1914, and he had written in it three other Housman poems.

GRANT RICHARDS

I met an acquaintance who had returned to England from Central America. The war, he told me, had so affected his affairs out there that he had no recourse but to return home. "And what are you doing with yourself?" I asked. He said: "I am staying down at a military encampment near London, reading *A Shropshire Lad* to the soldiers, and, by gad! don't they love it!" Many of the poems in *A Shropshire Lad* move to the sound of bugles, and all of them are robust. . . . Housman's soldier is brave in the great spirit.

HOLBROOK JACKSON

When I was on a visit to the front in France and Belgium during the war, one of the volumes of verse that were greatly in demand among the soldiers was *A Shropshire Lad*. It is not so curious as it may seem at first blush that *A Shropshire Lad*, with its philosophically pessimistic outlook, should appeal to those men who had been in the firing line. . . . For what is loosely called its pessimism is not so much that as a courageously stoical acceptance of the stern facts of human experience. The soldier was in no mood, just then, for gracious sentiment . . . , and the honest facing of the truth in *A Shropshire Lad* must have strengthened him to endure the fate that is, in the long run, common to all men.

A. ST. JOHN ADCOCK

The poet here faces his tragic conclusions with so fine a courage that it makes the book, when all is said, an inspiring one. The truth is that despair is no longer despair when it ceases to be dumb. Perfect expression purges despair of its own disastrousness and transfigures it into a mood that knows not only to endure, but even to delight.

JOHN DRINKWATER

To those of us [who were] at Princeton . . . in 1922 . . . Housman came as a discovery. Soon we knew all the poems of *A Shropshire Lad*, and quotations from them became part of our everyday speech. The simple verses were easy to remember and had a grave, haunting beauty which would not be denied. . . . Housman's wisdom was a bitter brew, but it did not inspire bitterness or despair.

NEILSON ABEEL

To say that a man is at once a poet and a pessimist is to be guilty of a contradiction in terms. Every work of art is an affirmation; your true, thorough-going pessimist would never think it worth while to create anything. Any person who is willing to take the trouble and risk of writing and publishing a volume of poems is optimistic enough for me. The more fine poetry there is in the world the less reason there is for quitting it. . . . Meditations upon death are nothing new, but *A Shropshire Lad* wears it cypress with a difference. . . . The poet's sureness of touch calls for our praise. . . . He has made war upon the ubiquitous adjective, and concentrated upon the bare noun and verb until they have done most of the work. . . . Notwithstanding his notable restraint . . . , his adjectives, when they come, are not the least of his minor felicities. . . . They are indeed sparkling little gems.

J. B. PRIESTLEY

Since 1896 all catholic lovers of poetry have known that there is one pure, small sound that can never be silenced—the flute of the Shropshire Lad. EDMUND GOSSE

Housman was a great poet. His range was limited, but there is not much reason for complaining that a violin has only four strings. Within that range he was very nearly perfect. EUGENE DAVIDSON

Another man, whom I met in Providence, had manufactured during his life a depressingly large number of braces—those articles which in America are whimsically termed "suspenders." We sat in the same hotel, while I informed him of the braces situation in Europe. He was not very interested until he learned, from a chance remark, that I wrote books. And then a light came into his eyes. He . . . produced . . . a first edition of *A Shropshire Lad*, which he knew by heart. I have seldom heard poetry recited so beautifully. BEVERLEY NICHOLS

In this small volume there are many flawless stanzas and not a few flawless poems. HUBERT BLAND

No book of verse published in the past half-century has attained a greater popularity than *A Shropshire Lad*.

MORTON D. ZABEL

Housman is one of the few living poets [in 1923] who know how and just where to end a poem.

WILLIAM ROSE BENÉT

Housman's language is entirely simple, but his simplicity is that of the cultivated and thoughtful mind.

HAROLD WILLIAMS

The simple ballad quatrain would seem to be the prevailing verse form, yet there are actually a large variety of stanza forms, in each of which is shown a diversity of rhyme schemes. . . . Because of his unerring but unobtrusive craftsmanship, . . . it is easy to understand the hold Housman has on his readers. RICA BRENNER

Our literature has produced little to compare with the perfect craftsmanship in the lyrics of A. E. Housman.

HENRY W. WELLS

A Shropshire Lad has steadily grown in favor and influence until it has quietly taken its place as one of the minor classics of our literature. One has only to mention *A Shropshire Lad* in any group of poetry lovers to see eyes light up and hear favorite bits lovingly quoted. . . . Housman uses twenty-one different measures in the sixty-three poems. It is quite true that he is fond of the octosyllabic . . . but he has few poems wholly in octosyllabic verse. To be exact there are thirteen. . . . It is doubtful if any other English writer uses so high a percentage of words of one syllable, slightly over eighty-four per cent. . . . Only one per cent of the words are three syllables. . . . Housman is the poet of a temperament. To an increasing number he makes a peculiar appeal. His thought is today in what Arnold calls "the main stream of ideas." Whether this explains his influence I am not sure, . . . but I am sure that with the exception of Thomas Hardy, no living poet has had such an effect on the work of his fellow-craftsmen. Echoes of *A Shropshire Lad* are everywhere, from Masefield to Edna St. Vincent Millay. . . . Housman's place in English literature seems to me as secure as that of his spiritual kinsman, Thomas Gray.   J. F. MACDONALD

It will be said that Housman is not a "great poet" because he has written no long poem. But his little poems are no carved cherry-stones. They hold in simple, imperishable perfection of form the simple, imperishable feelings of all humanity.

THE LONDON *Times*, AFTER HOUSMAN'S DEATH ON APRIL 30, 1936